Caliche Road Poems

Caliche Road Poems

David Meischen

LITERARY PRESS
LAMAR UNIVERSITY

Copyright © 2024 David Meischen
All Rights Reserved

ISBN: 978-1-962148-03-0
Library Of Congress Control Number: 2024931236

Lamar University Literary Press
Beaumont, Texas

These words are for my grandmother and my parents—
Lillie Bruns Meischen, April 6, 1896 – June 12,1979
Valerie Morgenroth Meischen, February 25, 1928 – May 13, 1995
Elwood Meischen, September 30, 1924 – March 7, 2015

and for my inimitable cousin—
Gary Meischen, August 11, 1948 – May 2, 1982

*They say time changes all it pertains to.
But . . . memory is stronger than time.*
   ~ Merle Haggard

Contents

A Note from the Author

Breath Against a Windowpane

1	As on the First Day
2	Another Kind of Answer
4	Untethered
5	Canning Day, 1955
6	Valerie
8	Hühnermusik
9	In the Cow Shed
10	No Footsteps, No Whispers, No Creaking Floorboards
11	Butcher Day
12	At the Bridge Railing Over the Gorge
14	Long Walk Home
15	Beneath Feathered Covers
16	The Garnett Translation
17	This Boy
18	No Man's Land
19	I forget he's there—

Even Whiskey

23	Moments from the Dance
24	On a Barstool at the Double Down
26	Self-Portrait with Elizabeth Taylor and Montgomery Clift
28	Season of the Drag Planter
29	Undone
30	Tusks
31	Cotton Harvest, 1962
32	Fever Dream
33	Darkest Evening of the Year
34	Reprieve in Three-Four Time
36	Hold Me, Darling, for a Little While
37	Death Wish
38	Wild Nights
40	Hurricane Force
41	Itch
42	The Vault

This Rainless Earth

- 45   What Holds You Here
- 46   The Algebra of Chance
- 47   What Survives Them
- 49   A History in Footsteps
- 50   Testament
- 51   Grit
- 52   His Hands Know How to Do It
- 54   Cotton Harvest, 1949
- 55   Requiem
- 56   Walking South Texas
- 58   The Rest is Silence
- 59   After the Harvest: Tractor, Stalk Cutter, Disk Harrow
- 60   Newborns Feeding
- 61   A Chill Like Sunlight Wakes Him at the Mirror Dreaming
- 63   Midsummer Morning
- 64   He Wanted a Straightedge Life

Is There an After?

- 67   Weather Marks
- 69   Frayed Thread
- 70   Here and Gone
- 72   Among the Stones
- 74   Letter from One Still Counting
- 76   Vanishing Point, 1949
- 77   Summer of a Lonesome Farmer
- 78   Qué Será, Será
- 79   High Cotton
- 80   The Shapes of Hats
- 81   Shortly Before the Last Day
- 82   Dreams of My Mother, 1995
- 84   Dry Spell
- 86   Months Later, He Rises from a Nap
- 87   Pegasus Leaping

Lesser Notes

Acknowledgments

In Appreciation

A Note from the Author

These poems originate from a particular place and time—the Meischen family farm in the Dilworth community of Jim Wells County Texas, 1948 and the years that followed. Locals knew where the farm was. Folks from elsewhere got lost trying to find us—along a county road about ten miles west of Orange Grove, where I attended school. If our county roads had numbers back then, they weren't marked by signs. We had a rural route and box number, no physical address. Years after I departed, some official entity assigned the farm a number on County Road 226. Using this identifier, Google Maps misplaces the farm by almost a mile.

Forty-some miles inland of Corpus Christi Bay, air on the farm is saturated with Gulf humidity. The feeling is tropical. The look is arid—brush country stippled with prickly pear and yucca, cenizo and agarita, huisache and mesquite. Agua Dulce Creek marks the farm's southern border, and like all creeks in South Texas, it is a dry creek—no water except when it rains, and rain is intermittent at best. When I got grown, I used to joke that only stubborn folk such as my German forebears would have arrived in such a landscape and said, "Hmmm. Let's have a farm here."

Breath Against a Windowpane

As on the First Day

Hackberries bend the light, clumped scrub
    beneath them prodigal with edge and thorn,
        dust sifting cool and fine between bare toes.

The lead cow found her way here
    fifty years ago, the others plodding
        after. You want to follow

as on the first day, not knowing
    the twists and turns beyond, just
        agarita, huisache, mesquite, the dapple

of shadow and sun, ahead
    the stir of something cryptic—
        like an alphabet for mockingbirds,

their vibrant language jumbled—
    a voice not quite remembered,
        the lilt of German dancing easy

Texas vowels, bright chorus
    of Grandma and her widow friends
        at home over coffee and cake.

Imagine breath against a windowpane.
    Touch the vapor warm against the cool
        glass, step back and watch your fingerprint

for the moment that it lasts, the imprint
    of breath against the reedy
        instrument humming in her throat:

Gone. Except in dreams that yield
    to waking stillness, to mossy branches
        sifting ambered afternoon, pools of paleness

lapping the shade here, a trail
    unfurling homeward through
        bottomland silt of the Agua Dulce.

Another Kind of Answer

i.
They watch the day's late sun wash over
the barn wall, the broken eggs. Elwood squats,

Judith and David perched on his knees, his arms
enclosing them. He asks *Why?* and they say
'Cause. Again: *'Cause why?* *Just 'cause, Daddy.*

Even at three and five, they understand what not
to tell their father: that they jumped and clapped

and wiggled each time an egg hit the wall:
'Cause it was fun, Daddy! But he so clearly
wants another kind of answer they forget

as only children who want to please
their father can forget the joy of breaking eggs.

It's a knotty question for him—no
comfort in the waste of a dozen eggs
to the simple pleasure of breaking them.

Drought saps the land he tills, the time
he spends posting checks at the bank

in town to make ends meet. He has a wife,
a second son napping in the house and—
dreaming in the womb—another son, the last.

ii.
Elwood can hear his mother laughing, saying
Let it go. Count your blessings. He remembers

escaping her strictures, he and his impish
brothers, wild toddlers climbing out
of their chicken-wire playpen to rush among

cotton pickers reaching for puffs of white
that dazzled them among swaying leaves.

His mother kept a secret from her sons:
that children can surprise you into rage
so sudden you can only let it loose

as laughter. Sometimes tears had come
first, and she told the story funny after.

But Elwood won't let himself cry. He is
too spent this afternoon to kindle anger's
heat, too played out to feel laughter itching

like a thistle in his throat. Asking *why*
and *why* and *why* is the best he can do.

When cool and shadow merge,
he hikes David to his hip, takes Judith
by the hand, and walks them to the cistern

for a bucket of water. Together, they wash
egg yolk, egg white, eggshell from the wall.

The hour thick with dusk and dimming
sun, they walk to the house for supper,
sparrows in the hackberries calling them home.

Untethered

for Kathy Stehle, February 20, 1949 – May 30, 1951

Swings squeak and hush, squeak,
hush again. Sunlight glances the chains,
swing and swinger arcing: *Higher, swing me higher.*

Mockingbird jubilates leaf-filtered morning sun,
sings *higher swing me higher.* Little girl laughs lighter
       —chain-link yearns toward weightlessness, sky.

Morning collapses—lurch and tumble—
elation fractured sudden as swing-frame pipe,
birdsong ruptured, breezes fading, fragile as breath

       —little girl flown away
somewhere, ragdoll flopped beneath a sprawl
of chains and pipe. So little left to mourn and bury.

Canning Day, 1955

Mother told you to watch the dial.
And left you to tremble. Flames purr
beneath the pressure cooker. Glassware

trembles in the cabinets, animated
by currents shivering the needle on the gauge,
the arc of its face incised beneath glass

in tiny exact measures and a band of red.
Like insect antennae calibrated
to bedrock's fissured pressures,

the needle ticks toward the edge of red
that means . . . what? A rush of light and heat
like that day the pilot light went out?

Mother crouched at the broiler door
reaching with her left hand to press
the pilot button, a match in her right.

You heard the match rasp
and a bright hot second later,
Mother unstrung against the far wall,

dark downy hairs on her forearm gone
and a smell like singed chickens
at the back of your throat, festering.

She didn't see it coming. You mull that over
watching flame flow against metal
like water translated into light.

Valerie

On Monday mornings, a fire smoldered
under the blackened kettle up by the wash-line,
and with the four of us circling, you went to work,

stoking the washer with a week's worth
of clothes, one load at a time, feeding them
through the clamorous wringer into the first rinse tub

and then into the second, with a bluing
tub for white things somewhere in between,
then out to the clotheslines, three of them

stretched along the outer yard, sagging under
sheets towels dresses shirts pants socks—and
a scorpion lurking one washday in the clothespin bag.

When one of Daddy's calves bellowed
from sunrise one Monday morning, penned
away from the teat, yawping for breakfast,

with a few clipped syllables you sent me to cut
a few stalks of grain to quell the racket. When
I whacked myself in the foot, my fear of bleeding

and lockjaw shrank before the greater fear
of disturbing you on washday. I wrapped
the bloody mess in brown paper and sulked out of sight.

When the wringer broke, you rolled your sleeves
and wrung our clothes by hand. Mrs. Elwood Meischen,
you always signed your name, but Momma,

you were always Valerie, always you, tenacious
as brush-country agarita—hair pulled back, forehead
misted with sweat, wrestling with children diapers laundry

cooking cleaning . . . pigs chickens cows crops work
and more work wearing at you but you would not give in
and when finally we grew out of diapers and

dependence and you got over the decade
you'd lost to motherhood's dizzying monotony,
no wonder that from thirty to forty you aged

into a younger version of yourself, not
the smiling teen-bride of your wedding photo,
with that jaunty spray of white feathers in your hair,

but you, Mother, dancing with Daddy to an old Glen Miller tune
or quietly fingering your rosary beads, a survivor's pride
in you, to have done what you set out to do.

Hühnermusik

Mornings we throw table scraps over the back fence. Coffee grounds and potato parings. Eggshells, banana peels, wilted lettuce leaves. Mornings *die hühner kommen*, cloud-white clusters—*fette weiße Vögel*. Clucking, carmine-crested, crimson-wattled, they scratch at our leavings, peck for tender grubs down in the dust. Sometimes the hens stop pecking, stop scratching, and flap. Little breaths of breeze jitter with their fluttering wings, our morning *gesprenkelt* by the diffident bursts of melody hens make for the sake of hearing each other at the task of being hens.

    percolator burbling
    polka rollicks the radio

In the Cow Shed

The water glows like carnival glass,
lush green of algae slicking the trough.
Bare-chested, the boy dips his pail.
Sky ripples in the silvered water,

the trough slick and lush with algae green.
Barefoot, the boy crosses to Brindle.
Overhead, unrippled, a silver sky.
He enters the smell of feed inside the shed,

bare-legged, talks to Brindle
while all around flies hover and hum—
they enter the spell of feed inside the shed.
Squatting, the boy splashes her udder.

The flies hover and hum, they hover and hum,
stippling shadows around Brindle's lively tail.
She swats. Hands splash her udder clean
and the boy steps back, sloshing. He flings the water,

packed earth stippled beyond Brindle's lively tail—
an arc held and falling, thrumming in the dust,
echo of his sloshing, spray of water flung.
He milks her then and ducks the rhythms of her tail,

milk held and falling, thrumming in the pail.
Summer scent of hay and milk foam, sweet and warm.
The boy grips and squeezes, he ducks the rhythmed tail
as the milk pail sings, Brindle humming in her bones.

Summer scent of grain, of foaming milk. Sweet
and warm, the boy fills his pail, bare-chested.
Milk sings against tin, Brindle humming in her bones.
The morning glows like carnival glass.

No Footsteps, No Whispers, No Creaking Floorboards

Outside the open window,
October shade. A collie yawns.

Beneath farther mesquites, cows
drowse, their skull bones humming.

Somewhere overhead
an airplane engine fades

into stillness. Gravestones
etched with names of the voiceless.

A neighbor's daughter struck
beneath a falling swingset, another's son

surprised by the depth of a stock pond.
Enthralled. Alone. They do not wake.

A fly stitches calm at the window screen,
wings buzzing with the pulse inside your ribcage.

Butcher Day

The pig snuffles at the fence, unfed,
hungry though not yet blood-hungry,

November morning cool and dry, a ghost
of summer's stench wafting up out

of dust where the pig waits, snout
pointing at the rifle barrel gleaming

down at him as Daddy aims and steadies.
Silence ruptures, a single staccato beat

rebounding against my chest and the pig
stalls: a gathering of will into the eyes,

rigid insistence against the loss engulfing
flesh and then—another blow to my chest—

the eyes drain flat as unoiled iron. Daddy
leaps the fence. A knife blade glints. Blood

—not spurting like a punctured jugular—but
sloshing, a bountiful wave slashed from the fatted

throat. The pig spasms, the blood puddle
congealing already at the edges, red-black and

darkening, powdered with dust from Daddy's
quick steps and the pig's hooves in their mockery

of running tipped over, his carcass flecked with
rusty spatters, his eyes blind to the cold gray sky.

At the Bridge Railing Over the Gorge

Far below, the Rio Grande.
A murmur. Serpentine.

Depth dizzies him, a catch
in his chest like a fishhook reeling

him   up   out   down
into inverted sky   tumbling

     long enough to measure terror.

A semi rumbles onto the bridge.
Beneath his feet, steel girders tremble,

transport him. A patch of brick-hard
dirt back home when he was four.

Salt cedars, smokehouse, fishpond.
Fading fence boards. Gate. On the other side,

     a rooster—baneful beak and bristling tail.

Pale, bare-chested, puffed up, the boy
shakes the gate at the rooster, feels the gate

shiver in his pulse—in his bones—
giddy with daring. Staggered.

Gate between them, the rooster puffs
breast feathers, brandishes his serrated comb—

     battle flag red as blood against rainless dust

—neck ruff, wing flap, spurs.
The boy rattles the gate against

chain-link gate-latch, jounces
the bent nail hooking chain-link

to gatepost. He shakes
once too often, once too wildly.

    Chain-link slips loose. The gate swings open.

He is back to himself
on the bridge, a flutter like wings

in his ribcage, hands
a fisted grip—semi clear

of the bridge, tremor fading
to a buzz in the balls of his feet—

    rooster loose in memory, no gate between them now.

Long Walk Home

golden shovel on a line by Carl Phillips

Caliche makes the road glow in the dark.
This boy ambles through an hour that
cools him, bathes him, renders
him faultless. Slowing, he does not fear shadow.
Unafraid, he embraces yearning, embraces all—
impervious to judgment. *But-but-but,*
the others would say. Meaningless,
their censure. Instead, this road, its glimmer—like
the lightest touch of fingertips, like the quietest song.

Beneath Feathered Covers

On the windowsill at dawn,
a glass of water glazed with ice.
Daddy will wake soon and strike
a match to the heaters. Until then,
the quiet rooms, the spill of morning gray.

The Garnett Translation

Snowflakes drop like rose petals
flowering Napoleon's armies—Moscow saved
by burning, Russia protected by its shroud of cold.

You've fallen in love with Natasha Rostov
in the pages of the British translation, Tolstoy's Russia
rendered in the voice of Austen and Brontë—

brisk as your glass of lemonade. A splash
of sunlight grazes your hand beside the glass,
rich tracery of veins, pale watercolor hue

of blood too visible on the back of a hand otherwise
so smooth. Natasha Rostov is smooth and cool
and silky, pale as the sheer white curtains

at the window where Grandma sits knitting,
hands flecked with brown, skin loosened
by age, translucent, networked with veins.

One of her pies is cooling in the kitchen—
butter, sugar, cinnamon—summer scent of peaches
wafting into a St. Petersburg drawing room. Grandma

talks while she knits. Her stories transport you
to her father's world, his Niedersachsen roots.
For a little while you close your book, close your eyes

and listen. Her stories are pages for you, too,
her life shaped by the language she was born to,
by hard times she weaves into wonder as she speaks.

Her knitting needles click the while, rhythmic
as the pulse that beats invisibly in her veins
and yours. You return to a landscape irreducibly

Russian, a voice British as afternoon tea,
surrender to daydreams of Natasha and the Rostovs,
French epaulettes against a field of snow.

This Boy

Inside a room that Sleeping
Beauty might have dreamt
my father's rules do not apply.

Lana and Marilyn have their own
bathroom with a bright-lit vanity
mirror and frou-frou vanity chair.

They have lipstick and mascara,
Barbies and a record player,
the Beatles and the Rolling Stones.

One of the Barbies sheaths herself
like Jackie Kennedy in lipstick-red bright
as the blood on her pink suit that day in Dallas.

We dance. Untethered. We morph a dozen
different steps. We pony and gallop, twist
and swim, jerk and double-jerk, jounce

ourselves breathless doing the hully gully.
Out back the boys are doing what boys do,
grunts and shouts penetrating the walls

of our shelter, so unlike courteous, cultivated Ken,
so unlike the girly boy, the Barbie in me.
Out back the boys roughhouse while I tease

Lana and Marilyn into perfect Bubblecut Barbies,
pursing my lips to say *bouffant*—like blowing
a kiss—at home in my dream at the end of the world.

No Man's Land

Pantywaist, he might have said. *Why don't you go inside? The Barbies are waiting.* What I remember is this: I let loose with my tongue, and Gary backhanded me.

> mulberry season
> faces purpled with juice

Pain pulsed in my jaw. Pain shot up my nose, singeing the corners of my eyes. For an instant, I was pure rage. I lunged and locked my teeth into the flesh of my cousin's chest.

> taste
> of the forbidden
> what I dared not name

By the time I entered high school, my cousin—a grade ahead—no longer bullied me, and I had learned to deflect the wisecracks he aimed at everyone. Years later, wondering how I sailed through high school unscathed, I remembered Gary was there. If any of the ruffians who walked the hallways with us, if even one of my badass cousin's blustering buddies had insulted me, harassed me, tried to push me around—Gary would have stepped in, fists raised.

> a wink and a grin
> teaching me to inhale

I forget he's there—

        the nine-year-old inside me
        clamoring to get out. Yesterday
for the space of minutes he got loose

                —playing me—

his giddy glockenspiel
   —delirious scales
      ringing
         my ribcage.

For others he has often
   been too much —   too
     many words flung out

              —decibels piercing—

pace a dizzy blur: he whirls
   inside a filament spun of humming,
     a jump-rope gyre   —   boy and lasso become

one
      boy become motion
    breath
breathless · ness
        —exultation—

                    yanked
by a word the other boys
             brandished.

The nine-year-old doesn't forget.
      He's carving his name inside my chest,
         one rib at a time.

Even Whiskey

Moments from the Dance

We danced past midnight, summer sweating us
like bourbon's smoky dare, Gulf breeze swirling
through dance hall windows, a tincture of salt
and sea to cool the evening heat, darken
into something like desire, its promise
of kisses languorous as slow dancing
against the keen serenade of steel guitar.

We cooled ourselves outdoors beneath light bulbs
strung from post to post, bottle caps surging
at our feet, scattered there like sand to crunch
beneath our dancing shoes while bartenders
dispensed us bottles wet with ice, tossed caps
upon the glinting record of our passing.

On a Barstool at the Double Down

This one is for Gary Meischen, with thanks to Buck Owens, Dwight Yoakum, Ray Price, Merle Haggard—all the sad jukebox voices.

Excuse me. I think I've got a heartache—
a bruise so deep tonight that even whiskey
cannot cure what's hurting me. Even you.
When you came back, you never meant to stay,
left me swayin' on this barstool. Nothin' but blue.
Close up the honkytonks, lock all the doors—

board up my cryin' places, nail shut the doors
that I keep stumblin' through. Stop up this heartache—
surely I can't take another day. Been blue
so long, don't need another shot of whiskey,
another migraine morning. Wish that I could stay
this hankerin', live easy just one day without you

drumming on my temple bones. Without you,
let me wake to sunshine, let me walk right by the doors
that draw me here. Give me a place where I can stay
awhile, a pier along the Cayo, where heartache
is a distant throb. No siren song of Seagram's,
but seagulls swooping overhead—an afternoon with skies so blue

the blues will drift away, the Bay a mirror, deepest blue.
If only for a minute I could break away from you.
Instead, this walled-in neon glitter, the wink of whiskey
warmin' where I hurt, jukebox tunes a maze of mirrors, doors
and more doors, voices callin', drenched in heartache,
voices sayin' *Hang on to your hurt*, voices sayin' *Stay*.

Really, though. Please don't make me stay
inside this boozy loop a minute more. I'm sick of blue,
can't hear another song that makes this old heart ache.
But then *my shoes keep walkin' back to you.*
I drop a quarter in the slot, play *Swingin' Doors*
and sing along, smoke-filled, doused in whiskey

regret. Bartender pours again, says *You know whiskey
cures what ails you. Have another. Have a double. Stay
awhile.* At five, I stumble through the doors
and out into a night just tilting into dawn, a hint of blue,
ink-wash blue lifting the sky, and right then I'm free of you.
The quiet whispers *No more heartache.*

The whiskey purrs *Let go of blue.* Crosswalks
wink like closing doors. I feel myself release you.
My heartache murmurs *Wonder if I'm here to stay.*

Self-Portrait with Elizabeth Taylor and Montgomery Clift

1961
When magazines passed their sell-by date, I pulled
them off the rack. Her face was on so many covers—

imperious brows, eyes lined dark as charcoal,
shadows in opaque blue-gray. Wedgwood

with an iridescent glaze—my million-dollar Cleopatra,
pneumococcal bacteria swimming in her lungs.

A scalpel saved her—tracheal incision, tube inserted
to carry breath while she hovered at the edge of gone.

1955
My mother cried, Aunt Madeline cried
at *The Last Time I Saw Paris*. I was six,

stupefied by her face in close-up, the violet
in the iris of the eyes that found me in the dark.

I remember snow, a locked door,
Van Johnson passed out drunk inside while

Elizabeth Taylor stood outside knocking.
My mother cried. Aunt Madeline cried.

1956
On a balmy night in May, she climbed
through the back window of a shattered car,

pulled herself over the bloodied seat and
cradled Montgomery Clift's wrecked face

in her lap. She reached into his throat
and removed broken teeth that choked him.

Distance, dark, and curving canyon roads
delayed the ambulance while Los Angeles spangled

the valley below, Monty's pain soothed
by the whispered words she breathed on him.

1962
I was thirteen and then fourteen, sorting
magazines, bagging groceries at the ice house.

I rang up beer and chew for a working cowboy
who sometimes slouched the aisles. One day he slapped

the new issue of *Look* on the counter—a close-up
of her famous face. *Get a load of those lips*, he said.

She cocks my trigger. When I looked at her,
my eyes said *beauty*. But the cowboy—leather

and sweat, hair curling from the V at his collar,
his grin when I look at him. My body says I *want*.

1956 and Later
After plastic surgery, Monty was back on set
with Elizabeth, his mouth no longer smiling,

voice a register of suffering. His face was never
quite the same, left side a crude stone rendering

of Matthew Garth's easy cowhand insolence,
riding herd in *Red River*. Pain gentled him

for a cowboy scene to come, hatted Monty
inside a phone booth, an aged misfit looking caged

behind a glass panel reinforced with chicken wire.
His squint is lonely in close-up. His gaze takes in

distance. Loss. Wrecked beauty, beauty nonetheless.
I look and look. I want to be touched by his longing.

Season of the Drag Planter

Hour upon hour I cat-walk the framework of two-by-ten boards atop this ramshackle apparatus: three wide-spaced steel-spoked wheels, rims like outsize barrel hoops, four plowshares to open rows for seeds, four spindly gearshift handles I manipulate to adjust plowshare depth in the soil seething below. Seed-bearing cannisters rotate on gear disks turned by the planter's axle. Two tiny plowshares cover the dropping seed. Bouncing along behind, four small rubber-flapped wheels tamp the seed beds. Daddy drives the tractor, short-tethered to impatience. I monitor the planter. I long for the waving cup towel that signals supper on the table.

    rusted couplings
    abrade the eardrum
    dust-choked dreams

Undone

Rain the night before, the cowpen puddled, ankle deep
in mud sucking at my rubber boots, young cow in this pen,
her calf weaned away in the next while Herman danced at the fence,
flop-eared pup, best dog we ever had. Ahead, the cow's back end,
a flashing blur—she startled, who knows why—her hooves
tracing an arc in the light, a muddy smear on my chest, my jaw.

After supper Daddy sat with his hands folded on the table,
knuckles knobby as burls where two fingers were missing.
He had news from town. Neighbor's boy, thirteen years old.
Tractoring a shredder over grain stalks. *Must've fallen
asleep*, Daddy said. *Or turned to check the shredder.
Lost his balance. They wouldn't let his momma into the field.*

Herman woke us barking. Outside the bedroom windows, a coiled
rattler, Daddy out the back door with his sixteen-gauge—
sound waves resounding between the house and the butane tank,
the blast in my chest. Awake afterwards, I remembered
a family story decades old—Grandma's sister weeding the garden.
Big snake struck her hoe handle, fang marks at eye level.
In bed for days, Grandma said. Sick with *what if*.

Forty years apart from the farm, I wake one night,
nothing left of my dream but the moment that woke
me—my jawbone crunching, brittle bone crumbling
under impact. Odor of rain, mud, manure, hay. My brain
not ready yet to wake, synapses signaling *broken, broken, broken*.

One morning Herman wasn't at the back door waiting.
We called and called. No sign of Herman. We found him
beneath a mesquite tree, that lacy dappled shade,
fang marks on his swollen jaw. Herman breathing
his last. Beneath a live oak not twenty yards away, blood-pocked,
a slumped diamondback—roadrunner pecking at her fresh kill.

Tusks

From the feed room at the back of the barn, the boy passes a row of pomegranates in bloom, brushstrokes of sun-shot red. Cool this morning, with a hint of coming heat in the smell of hay stacked for the cows. The pigs are ready to be fed, snouts at the wire-strung pen.

    backstrap
    dredged and fried
    butcher day knives

Near the fence separating the pigs from the sheep, a ragged splotch of white. The boy sees what's left of a lamb that wriggled through the flimsy fence wire. Legbones haphazard, blood shining wetly where the abdomen has been ripped open, intestines in a useless scramble. The boy turns from the gutted lamb, walks back toward the pigs. They nose at the corn, grunting, contented. They look harmless. He studies their canines.

    remembering
    sharp-toothed rage
    his cousin's sweet blood

Cotton Harvest, 1962

Midday apparition: a figure pale as sunlight,
her skirt billowing above sun-blazed green.
You are soaked in your own liquid, your flesh

like candle wax, salt stiffening in your shirt.
At row's end your sack is weighed and water
never tasted so good. The crew head records

the pounds you picked. Your sack is lifted up,
your cotton spilled onto the truck. Snatches
of song from the radio in the cab, a gaggle

of cousins around the open door. Sacks empty,
they trade fancies about a couple on the dance floor
last night—the male six-four, his sweetie five-one.

I bet she has to stand on a chair when they do it.
The cousins chuckle and nudge. They turn to you,
winking. You turn away, step into mesquite shade,

open your lunch sack. Salami and crackers, an apple.
More water. You drowse. *Barbiturate overdose.*
Someone at the dashboard is turning the volume up.

Marilyn Monroe found dead. A burst of static.
Chloral hydrate, the newsman says. *Pentobarbitol.*
You stumble up, falter into trees along the creek,

thick live oak canopy where you unzip to piss,
a spasm yanking at your ribcage. Agarita bristles
nearby, sharp tips glinting in a thin beam of sun,

the breeze feverish. Her voice singing.
I prefer a man who lives and gives expensive jewels.
Her diamonds dazzle against hot pink satin.

Fever Dream

The diamondback disappears beneath
the farmhouse, naps through an August afternoon,

slithers into a silted creek bottom
canopied by massive oak trees weeping moss,

coils beneath yaupon holly—*Ilex
vomitoria*—berries glistening red as malice.

The diamondback drowses in hot shade,
poised and ready like a cat with a secret

—like envy or betrayal or any other
deadly sin I will not remember when I wake.

Darkest Evening of the Year

with gratitude to Robert Frost

I have outwalked myself tonight, walked out
in deepest dark and back, but not to say goodbye
or call you back. I brim with hurt tonight,
fragile as the leaves my feet crush where they drift.
You will not see me stopping here to watch this creek
fill up with night—no luminary moon to clock the sky.
Deep and dark down here beneath the oaks. Ahead,
beyond the bend, an interrupted cry comes over
treetops from a preying owl. The only other
sound: the sweep of unshod feet in downy silt.
I have outwalked myself tonight. Still miles to go
along this creek, miles to go outwalking sleep.

Reprieve in Three-Four Time

Dance wax scattered on the dance hall floor—
his right hand gentle at her skirt's back loop,
her right hand lifting to his raised left. They dance.
Cheek to cheek, this whirl. No tears for now.
The two-step did not mend them. Will the waltz?
And who said who was coming back to stay?

He said, she said. Chance is neither one will stay
beyond another bitter night, another clash. But the floor
skims beneath their whirling shoes. They could waltz
until daybreak—*one*-two-three, *one*-two-three—this loop
of heartache forgotten, only each other, only now.
Sweat glistens and cools on their cheeks as they dance,

dizzied, on this coupled carousel, dance
swirling them out of themselves, wishing they could stay
where disappointment cannot reach them, wishing now
would not be shattered, no morning headache, no floor
to break the feel of swooping. Already, though, the loop
is losing its hold. Tempo slows, fiddle fades, waltz

winding down. They stand among billowing skirts, the waltz
still in them, walls spinning. If only the dance
they do outside these walls were not a loop
of poisoned words, if only they could stay
inside the trance they spin by spinning on this floor.
They grin, they nuzzle noses, they swear this time now

will last. Luck, they know, is fickle. But now
and then it whirls them like the waltz
that leaves them breathless on this reeling floor.
Who's to say what song is next, what dance
step? *Play on*, he calls to the band. *Stay
with me*, she whispers. She prays the loop

of hope will hold. The music starts again, another loop
that dazzles. *Yes*, they whisper to each other. *Now*.
This time, surely, what they feel will stay
unsullied. They glide into the count. The waltz

embraces them—*one*-two-three, *one*-two-three. They dance
past midnight, belief beneath them, its shifting floor.

I'll stay, he whispers, a loop of promises,
as dance wax slicks the floor with magic.
The waltz is all they know. For now.

Hold Me, Darling, for a Little While

syllables of laughter tumble
    kaleidoscopic bourbon-staggered past
        midnight party-pummeled I stumble

to the balustrade old friend
    beside me in her wheelchair top step
        at my toes first note in a glissando spilling

I scoop her up take the first
    steps down one-two-three-four-five I lose
        my balance her weight less than nothing my

feet choppering risers balusters treads falling
    and trying always to fall upright arms
        cradle her above my falling
            limbs holding her falling
                and she falling
                    with me

        through flickering
            lamplit Gulf-wet
                cricket song
                      to the landing:
                                    Safe.

~ ~ ~ ~ ~

        That was more than fifty years ago.
        My friend died when the muscles working
her lungs finally gave out. I call across a chasm

    to myself at nineteen, panting, panicked:
Breathe. You'll get to the end like your friends rollicking
stair-top. This moment unbroken will not save you.

Death Wish

One Sunday morning in 1974, I sat with Gary on the steps of the drive-in grocery and ice service that had fallen to him two-plus years before when a sudden stroke felled his father. My cousin was badly hung over that morning. The bags beneath his eyes, always visible during this stage of his life, had darkened like bruises. Hair uncombed, face ashen, shoulders slumped, characteristic bravado conspicuously absent—no glint of irony, no words to needle me.

    barstool blues

You look a wreck, I said. *If you don't take better care of yourself. What'll your life be like when you're forty?*

David, my cousin said, *I won't make it to forty.*

    such a beautiful dream

Gary was thirty-three when he died, coming home from a late night by himself at a club somewhere in Corpus Christi. He fell asleep at the wheel. His car sideswiped a freeway divider. He wasn't wearing a seatbelt.

    nobody's sugar daddy now

Wild Nights

i. January 1, 1970
Just past midnight four of us
made a Russian-style toast, smashed
our glasses against the wall of a shabby room
in Austin's West Campus, slivers embedding
in the carpet. I read aloud from Thomas Wolfe,
his words echoing across the years:
We were young and drunk and twenty
       and would never die.

ii. October 31, 1969
I crawled from the front passenger window
of my best friend's Plymouth Belvedere,
upside down, front bumper snubbed
into the dirt where we'd rolled it—unseatbelted,
whiskey sours on our breath—homebound
from a party out by the Balcones Fault Line.

Deep breaths of cool midnight air.

Unhurt. Not so much as a bruise,
a scratch, a sore muscle—either of us.

iii. September 2, 1962
I remember a single word, single
syllable from John Allen's funeral.
    No.

The rowdy ones had been out,
two cars abreast drag-racing
down a two-lane country highway
      —empty—
except for John Allen Herschap,
driving home in his Volkswagen.
Twenty-five years old. Only brother,
three sisters. He'd been to see his fiancée.

    No.

A bellow that howled
from a bottomless place.
A moan that sobbed. Sorrow.
                    All of sorrow
                                —ever—
cleaving inside John Allen's
father's rib cage.

Hurricane Force

The sky roils in him. He yearns
for ruin, renewal. A witness. How wind
can bend hackberries and mesquites, how the song
of tempest might promise rapture—tremors
rippling the ribcage, window glass awakened by rain

turned horizontal, a storm he cannot defy, rain
unleashed inside him. Like masted Odysseus he yearns
for wreckage. Rag towels, mop buckets. Day-dark trembles,
rain gauge useless, windows bleeding water, pummeled by wind.
His towels sop leakage into buckets, a tempo for the song

he has been swallowed by—a psalm
for water rising beneath floorboards. Ceaseless rain.
One moment a prayer for safety, the next to be shattered by wind,
his pulse throbbing along wrists and forehead, blood churning
while thunder shivers floor joists, furniture, glassware, each tremor

a contagion. Between gusts, trees upright, trembling
beneath leaden skies. Past surfeit, the creek croons
over the fields, the current a deep chord yearning.
In the breath after lightning, Thor's hammer reigns
outside and in. Deep in his throat, he rasps with the wind,

a ballad for Noah on waters muddied thick. And the wind
weakens. From every direction, frogs in full-throated tremor,
calling, calling, an answer thrumming in him, insistent as rain.
On the radio, between bursts of static, fragments of song,
rupture beyond rupture, the chorus of flood. Yearning.

He steps outside, stands trembling. No wind now, no rain.
He yearns and knows why. He aches to follow the song
unfurling inside. The waters whet. The waters do not quiet.

Itch

Amarillo by morning, up from San Antone. I
begin two-stepping in my kitchen alone, George Strait

crooning another lonesome cowboy ballad,
dancehall memories unfurling, smoke-hazed.

Every sliding solo step, every swirling pivot, every
fancy maneuver, takes me back to an August night.

Gruene Hall. Luchese boots, spit-shined. Dusky
hat brim rakishly tipped. Jeans so snug they made me

itch. I miss who I might have been. I miss
Jax beer iced so cold it made my teeth hurt,

khakis starched stiff as a wet-dream boner.
Lucifer moves in me tonight, knows how to tempt me—

makes me want a margarita—Cuervo Gold—murmurs
Numb yourself. Go ahead. Never stop at one. If

only the lie could make it so, the fall from
paradise reversible. One dancing tune, one drink alone cannot

quench the hunger roiling in me *when the cowboy
rides away*. Heard that song graveside once—

straight up made me cry. Wonder will I shed tequila tears
tonight, dance around the room alone some more. Mr.

Unrequited, feeling sorry for himself, certified
ventriloquist's dummy, full of jukebox heartache.

What am I to do, wanting whiskered kisses, triple
X tussles with a hairy-bellied bronco buster?

Yearning, I sip another margarita. I dream a man named
Zebediah. *Bestowed by God.* Would that he will come.

The Vault

*Jim Wells County, Texas, 1965,
at the intersection of Hwy 359 and FM 624*

Heavy thump muted by rubber edging—the door
behind you closing. Frigid clink of the inside

latch. Light bulbs caged along the ceiling,
incandescence dimmed by cold, by dark

seeping from the walls. Bars of ice lined up blank
as uncarved marble, three-hundred pounds apiece.

Gleam of depth, gleam of solid cold
laced with rime. Muffled murmur of refrigeration.

Beside you the crusher stands mute,
open-throated, a stilled gargle of teeth,

of tempered steel. Ice tongs dangle from
the crusher, ice pick stuck into slatted flooring,

your gloves useless these hours without end,
feeding chunks into the maw. Bagging, tying,

stacking. The chill seeps deep. When you push
to get out, the latch jams, your voice trapped

inside your rib cage, the words for help strangled,
shards in your throat. At the back of the vault, half-lit,

half-draped by dark, three gutted bucks. Curve
of ribs once animated by breath. Glisten of congealed fat,

striated sinews. Eyes twice glazed: by gunshot,
by cold's embrace. These gelid walls, this light

that will not light, the dusty grid of streets beyond—
even after you get away, this door will not unlock.

This Rainless Earth

What Holds You Here

Under late September sun, the new arrivals ponder this shallow soil.
Caliche hardpan, sifting bottomland silt—they wander this shallow soil.

These weathered Germans are blocked by thickets of thorns and spines.
As dark descends, they hesitate: *Was it a blunder, this shallow soil?*

Stubborn as their Niedersachsen roots, they clear cacti and scrub.
Fall and spring, mule and harness and plow sunder this shallow soil.

Dry seasons, sorghum seedlings sprout and shrivel. Even weeds wither.
Heat shimmers the glare as whirlwinds squander this shallow soil.

At seventy, eighty and beyond—Elwood walks the fields, feeds the cows.
Others ask, *What holds you here?* He points yonder: *This shallow soil.*

The firstborn son remembers: smoke house, hen yard, windmill, barn.
David—the Hebrew root cries *beloved*—his wonder, this hallowed soil.

The Algebra of Chance

Oma and Poppa gaze into the diminishing sun of a day at midcentury, eyes startled to have come this far, between them a glass-pedestaled cake in tiers of white topped by a number in crystallized sugar—50—behind them family members clearly conscious of aperture, shutter, film, among these Valerie, eight months a bride, and beside her Elwood, tall, handsome, radiant, young. From here they look like one set of variables in a three-part algebra problem—a point of departure, a destination, the distance between. Read closely; parse the givens; set a clock ticking. And arrive some two dozen years later: Valerie and Elwood stand behind a cake that says 25, a daughter and three sons, all grown, arrayed around them.

First of the sons, I consider my sister, her invisible presence five months before she was born, among the smiles backing Oma and Poppa, though my mother didn't know the child she carried on January 27, 1947, would be her only daughter. And what about me? I study my parents at eighteen and twenty-two, see myself—my father's mouth, my mother's smile—waiting just outside the frame, my entrance certain as Uncle Ewald, his absence an erasure among survivors.

See him there?—inside the deep porch shade, beside the door of the board and batten house they stepped out of to pose for us, afterimage of the beloved bachelor son. A single cell briefly in place inside Oma's womb, a random sperm among the myriad discharged at the instant of ejaculation—a chance collision brought Uncle Ewald into the family story, left him an immune system that weathered childhood illness, the hit-or-miss dispersal of 1918's deadly flu, and so on until January 7, 1945, when fluke landed a mortar shell in an army kitchen somewhere in Belgium, Uncle Ewald calmly peeling potatoes until a split second before the flash that killed him.

Not one of us was meant to be. Even seconds before the merging of two cells that led to me, I was not in the picture. Another sperm cell could have got there first. Or none at all. Out of happenstance, a family assembles itself. A child arrives. Another. The ones dumb luck lets in the door. We sit for photographs anyway, make—of the flux we are given—equations, the selves we cannot imagine otherwise.

What Survives Them

*after Mourning Picture—1890, oil on canvas, 28 X 36 inches—
by Edwin Romanzo Elmer*

i.
The child who died lives on, preserved
in pigments by her father. Remembered. Re-
embodied. The child and her lamb, the rattan stroller
nestling her doll. One hundred and thirty years later I gaze
at her red-ribboned hat orphaned on the grass, transmuted into
pixels, into light made visible as color. And back to the lamb, pale
hand at its collar, striped frock, pale face—an image of an image
of a child no longer breathing, her parents seated nearby, stiff
in mourning clothes, their love no proof against a burst
appendix, her name a whisper in the lilac shade. Effie.

ii.
My great-grandmother left no painting
of her youngest. Oma kept Ewald Morgenroth's room
instead, ashtray and pipe on a shelf set into the headboard,
uniforms hanging in the closet. Pressed. Waiting. I stood inside
this still life once, dust and silence coating every surface, Oma
gone to her grave, the old house leaning in on itself. A trunk
biding in the attic, her husband's wedding shirt folded there.
A Valentine card signed to my grandfather when he was a boy.

iii.
Julius Arthur Bruns is on my mind
this afternoon, my grandmother's beloved
brother. He peers from the one surviving photo,
a round-faced little boy, youngest of five, flanked
by Willie and Anton, clearly brothers—dark eyes, dark hair,
dark suits, silky bows tied loosely at the collar. Beside them,
stair-stepped all in white, Lillie and Adele, somber as their brothers.

Johann Wilhelm Bruns was not yet fifty when he stood with them—
curly hair, thick moustache, no hint of gray. He'd crossed the Atlantic
with his wife and daughters Anna, Frieda, Helene. Buried
his wife, married again, fathered the five gathered

here. Buried their mother. Assembled them today,
a father mourning inevitable loss: little Julius,
hands loosely fisted, holding on, his faulty
appendix keeping its secret. For now.

Like Effie, Julius does not smile.
Like his mother, he has no claim on lasting.

A History in Footsteps

Mornings on the farm, I woke
to my father's tread. *Better hear those feet
hit the floor before I get there.* Floorboards

groaned beneath footsteps, sinewed oak
a drumhead over sturdy joists, dark damp
space beneath. My grandmother walked

these floors. My father, his brothers.
My grandfather, gone before I breathed—
his steps sounded here. My great grandfather—

we called him Opa—paced the decks
of a ship crossing the Atlantic, steps
unsteadied by swells and troughs, unmoored

from his Niedersachsen footing.
I hear Opa saying *Boden*, solid as the floor
he named, steady as *Fußtritt, Hartholz*—

footsteps on hardwood—floors
he built himself, his voice in my ear
when I sat in his lap. I was four and Opa

was ninety. I loved the heft of O
in *Boden*, Opa's rounded mouth,
the O pouring forth, breath made audible,

B-flat sustained on the baritone horn
I played in high school, my foot keeping time
on the band hall floor, Opa breathing in me.

Testament

i.
Field dust, caliche, mesquite. A creek
named Agua Dulce by those who came
before, this creek adrift in bare dry silt
on a scrub-brush plain. Fathomless sky.
Wisps of cloud. Heat staggering the light.
Weeks—and sometimes months—before the rains came:
thunderstorm gully washer floodwater rains,
drown your cattle drown
your neighbor drown yourself rains.

ii.
We came from the quietude of dust,
from the windowpane tremor of thunder
and thirst. We stood in the rows of sorghum
and cotton and corn that sprang up
when the rains came and cooled us,
when the rains came and washed us clean.

Grit

i.
War has come. Two of Grandma's sons depart for the South Pacific. The third—my father—picks cotton beside his mother. Through ceaseless summer, through sunlight hazed by dust, Grandma goes on. Forty years a widow, thirty years with no one to muffle the hush of her house at night. She raises flowers that stagger us with color. She cooks and cans and sews for us.

> bluebonnet spring
> fresh turned earth
> of her garden plow

ii.
One day she speaks of getting too old to be useful. *I'll go to the old folks' home*, she says. *You will not*, I insist. *We'll take care of you*. I grab another ginger snap, turn back to *The Grapes of Wrath*. Too soon the cookie jar is full, the grandchildren elsewhere. I write letters from college. Grandma needs more than letters. Then one of her sons dies, forty-eight years old, felled by a stroke. Bitterness spills from her days.

> unoiled screen door
> jaybird jeering
> from hot shade

iii.
She lingers in her garden when I stop to say goodbye—leaving to start a life elsewhere. I walk out to the street, turn to gaze at her stooped figure arched against blank sky, whacking at the waste of weeds that choke her beds. I get into my car, my promise ringing in the silence. *We'll take care of you*. I drive to sea-salt Galveston and walk the seawall, the Gulf murky with hurricane threat.

> undertow chafes
> at the jetties
> her breath seizes

His Hands Know How to Do It

Elwood vaulted from the tractor seat, his boots crunching the brittle shell at the surface of the field. With the tractor idling, he could hear the day now—brittle cornstalks rustling with hot, dry gusts of wind, the sharp scree of birdcalls like surveyor's markers in the deep brightness above. The tractor engine puttered. The harvester clacked. The wind blew hot against his sweating, dust-encrusted face. The clots of shuck and stalk resisted, but Elwood had done this and done this and done this before. His hands knew how to do it, knew which piece of shuck or stalk to grasp, knew how to pull and discard, pull and discard, until the harvester would be clear again.

He saw his mistake before he felt it, saw what was coming in the split second before it was too late—his hand, his leather glove, the tips of the fingers of the glove, the leather molded by wear and sweat into a second skin, into protection against rough farm surfaces, against hours at the steering wheel of a balking tractor, turning and holding and holding and turning. Protection against barbed wire and prickly pear, against the scorpion's sting, the black widow's bite. In the split second that he knew it was too late, the tugging felt gentle. Like a whisper. Like Valerie's voice at his ear while they danced.

And then pain.

Pain stills a hot September wind, drops scissortails out of the sky. Pain banishes Valerie, banishes Elwood's mother, his brothers. Pain binds Elwood into flesh and bone at the tips of the fingers on his right hand. Pain explodes, its currents pulsing in his groin, his finger bones snapping beneath hard metal edges.

The harvester will stall when flesh and bone are thick enough to jam it. But Elwood is alone in the field. No one can save him. He does what he must, everything in him going tight against the pain—feet planted, legs bent, shoulders poised. Crouching, he pulls back with all his strength. New pain knifes through him. But the punishment that washed over him when the harvester bit into his fingertips was so far beyond the threshold of what a man can bear that now—when the second wave crashes down—he has been severed from himself. Pain is happening to someone else. Elwood feels instead the slide of leather against the knuckles of his right hand, feels the wiry hairs on the back of the hand tingle under the glide of leather, feels the illusion of cool as he pulls free of the glove and late-summer air moves along the sweaty surface of exposed skin. As if from elsewhere, he registers the arc of pain as the damaged hand catapults away from the clacking harvester. He feels the impact of his buttocks against the surface of the field, another wave engulfing him.

He is moaning now. He hears himself moaning, feels his right hand throbbing. He looks. Two of his fingers are gone—the forefinger, the middle finger—stumps pulpy and bleeding. The thumb is there. It looks like what's left of a lamb that has slipped into a pigpen by mistake. The fourth and fifth fingers are oddly intact.

Standing, Elwood yanks at shirt buttons with clumsy, left-handed fingers; he grasps the right side of his collar, lowers the shirt, pulls it down his forearm and over the damaged hand. Slouching his left shoulder, shaking his arm and hand, he drops the shirt into the dust and picks it up. He grapples the shirt into a bundle and in a single move presses it to the bleeding place where his fingers were. This time, he bellows with the pain. But he is safe. At the house there will be help. He turns and walks toward healing.

Cotton Harvest, 1949

At noon high sun, pickers gathered in the yard.
Hackberry shade, migrants descended from slaves.

Sardines dipped in mustard. Salt crackers. Water
cool from the can, clean taste of tin on the tip of the tongue.

Work shirts stained with salt, like watered silk,
collar bones deep-bruised from heavy, dragging sacks,

fingertips stippled by prick-sharp bolls. Chafed
knees, an ache in the small of the back. Throbbing.

Two-thousand pounds plucked out of the field
to make a bale, five hundred pounds when

the gin was done—each bale fetching a hundred.
We've got a bumper crop, Elwood said over supper.

Rain and sunlight that year—every row exploding
with bolls, every boll split open to white.

In the morning Valerie walked out to the field
with her Brownie box camera—the green

dark as charcoal in the pictures. Elwood
smiled between rows, the cotton chest-high.

Weeks later, up in the hackberry branches, a worn out
leather knee pad. No one thought to reach it down,

toss it in the burn barrel. Years flown by, the dried-up
leather, barely visible, grown into a cleft. In the field beyond

cotton sprayed with defoliant, mechanical harvester chewing up
the crop, rows of stalks behind—brittle, skeletal, choked with dust.

Requiem

Goathead sticker vines thirst
among the headstones, caliche rocks

like skulls beneath the unforgiving
edges—agarita, huisache, Spanish daggers—

this rainless earth barb-wired, boxed in.
Bone white of crushed rock on the lane

beyond, a lone roadrunner skimming
the indifferent heat, behind him a shimmer

veiled with dust. Undisturbed,
ants harvest a treaded horned toad—

stillness biding, sunlight rife—and among
the stones, a whirlwind, its brief promise.

Walking South Texas

*from the Rio Grande near Zapata to Agua Dulce Creek
in Jim Wells County*

Aquí se abre. Here an opening:
barbed wire clipped by some
coyote's wire cutters, barbed wire

spiraling from a shaggy, shedding
cedar post, a rattler curling
in the brush, vigilant even in sleep.

Aquí se abre. Hunger draws him,
the mirage of a new life: *el espejismo.*
Beyond this fence, another, another—

roadrunners, jackrabbits, javelinas leading
the way, bright dry day bleeding into cold
dry night: *antes y otra vez, otra vez, otra vez.*

One morning, a creek bed, cool and dry
and live-oak shaded. Another fence, a field.
Beyond the field, a gate, a yard, a bed: geraniums

red as the first fresh drops of blood.
A walkway strewn with pebbles. Foot scraper
and steps, weathered boards. A shaded porch:

chair, table, pitcher, the almost taste
of *agua y limonada.* A screen door opens,
lone farm wife stepping out of shade,

her husband in the field, she says, distant
murmur of a tractor where she points, dust
whorling there. Seedlings, rain, harvest—

these are hopes he knows too well.
Her eyes, though. Fence posts, barbed wire
that marked his way, the river he swam.

She wants him on the other side.
You have no place here, her eyes say.
Move along. But he will stay.

Trabajo, he says—a word, a need.
Work she clearly understands. The fields will take
what he can offer. *Aquí se abre.*

The Rest Is Silence

Elwood bends to the corner table, switches on the radio, a soft glow lighting its face as he turns the dial. Watery voices, garbled snippets of song spill into the quiet room. And then, a clear signal, his favorite lyric. A German river, a soldier's ballad, the lost Fräulein he sings to *each night when the stars start to shine.* Elwood settles into his listening chair. Overhead, deep beyond his imagining, Sputnik circles, spinning his world toward another brink.

    from the moonless dark coyote's mournful cry

After the Harvest: Tractor, Stalk Cutter, Disk Harrow

The light here on the screened-in porch is ever gray.
Hands cupped, he splashes cheeks cool and clean.
The screen door swings open, clatters shut.

Hackberries shade his walk across the yard—
inside the shed, the heavy, hulking tractor,
mute for now. Unmotored silence hums.

He idles the throttle, works the hitch, moves on:
his bones have memorized the rumble.
An hour on the tractor. Another. Another.

Headless sorghum falls beneath cleaving blades,
dust in a plume behind serried disks, slicing, slicing—
death quick and brutal if he should drowse and fall.

Death. Quick and brutal if he should drowse and fall,
dust in a plume behind serried disks, slicing, slicing.
Headless sorghum falls beneath cleaving blades—

an hour on the tractor—another, another—
his bones have memorized the rumble.
He idles the throttle, works the hitch, moves on,

mute for now, unmotored. Silence hums
inside the shed—the heavy, hulking tractor.
Hackberries shade his walk across the yard.

The screen door swings open, clatters shut.
Hands cupped, he splashes cheeks cool and clean.
The light here on the screened-in porch is ever gray.

Newborns Feeding

Blackie is indifferent this morning
to the damage she has done, her
hoofprint bleeding like a rose

on watered silk, the piglet
she stepped on wasting quietly
beyond the flurry she turns to—hunger

crying like a nest of raised beaks.
Swelling with milk, Blackie
tips her balance, piglets scattering

to the edges of her massive, listing figure,
the sudden flattening crush. She grunts
and piglets scramble at the nipples

stippling her belly, attach their mouths
expertly to root at this thirst, each mouth
nuzzling one glistening teat, a cluster

of mouths, a syncopation of suckle
and pull back, of tongue and nibble and
nudge, a rapture of tiny-throated grunting.

Off to the side, the damaged piglet breathes.
There is no movement otherwise, no sound above
the suckling. A brick will end his suffering.

A Chill Like Sunlight Wakes Him at the Mirror Dreaming

The scent of blood reaches the boy clean
and cold in the deep of his nostrils, the newborn

calf so newly gone he can feel the last breath
leave her, see the tremor of muscles relaxing

as her head sinks into creek bottom silt, her eyes
wide open, so quick was her coyote—her blood

bright on his snout—her coyote arrested where
he pounced, the boy arrested half-step watching,

handheld radio light as a pack of cigarettes pouring
words into his ear. *Somebody, somebody, somebody, please.*

Reflex answers for him, his thumb at the disc
for sound and power: a click and silence,

a click: the coyote startles, turns running,
turns again, regards the boy regarding him,

a gaze like sunlight through amber, the hush
deepening, dizzying, newborn heifer still as stone,

her eyes clouding beneath a blue without
measure, the sky so empty its bright heat chills—

and the boy turns. He eases away, a song
at his ear again, calf and coyote put behind,

voices embracing him: mother and brothers,
a girl—her smile—marriage, children, the years

tumbling, the distraction of noises. Then
one morning a face in the mirror, an old man.

In the room beyond, a woman curled in death,
eyes at half mast, clouding, and he remembers:

how the coyote looked at him and tasted
blood and waited. How patient the stillness.

Midsummer Morning

From his pillow, he considers the silent tractor,
bales of hay lined up in rows beneath the sun,
fields mowed and bleaching, dry and drier,
a sky devoid of clouds, forgetting blue.

The bales extend in rows beneath the sun,
no rain since May. Light tastes of dust today,
the sky devoid of clouds. Forget blue,
forget cool, forget rest, forget even

rain, none since May. Dust seasons the light
he breathes at the window, heavy in his bones.
Forget cool, forget rest, forget even
grace, a breath of breeze beneath the oaks.

His bones grow heavy. Here beside his window,
the end lingers, a persistent lumbar aching, patient as
a murmur in the breeze beneath the oaks.
Dust and shadow stir there: only penance, no relief.

The end resides in him, a patient ache, reminding him
death has no need of hurry, nowhere else to be but here,
where dust and shadow stir: only penance, no relief.
An hour, another, another, looking out this window,

nowhere to be but here. Death has no need of hurry.
The hay lies mowed and baled. It bleaches dry and drier.
An hour, another, another, he waits beside his window.
From his pillow he considers tractor, sunlight, silence.

He Wanted a Straightedge Life

i.
Hot breeze along the county road,
hackberry leaves fluttering. Daddy sent us
with grubbing hoes: *Clean 'em out.*

Barbed wire prickled taut from post to post.
Sparrows chattered along the top strand,
guts rife with undigested hackberry seeds.

Johnson grass choked the bar ditch.
Beneath the sparrows, hackberries shimmied,
seedlings one day, saplings the next,

a snaggle in the fence wires. Daddy
railed against seeded bird shit, meddlesome
trees bungling his perfect fence line.

ii.
Seven years Daddy's gone now. Yesterday
I turned into the county road, a mile-long
tunnel of dusted green, bar ditches snarling:

hackberries tangled with huisache bristling
alongside mesquite. At the dry low-water
crossing, a roadrunner spear-beaked a rattler.

We sons have gone elsewhere. Our father
lies beside our mother. And here, a flourish
of sparrows, of seeds, of every weedy thing.

Is There an After?

Weather Marks

i.
Julia's photo harks back to the century before mine. A matron stands beside a highboy, right elbow crooked to rest there, fingers of the left hand draped over her right wrist. The dress is severe, with a rich, dark sheen, set off by two rows of covered buttons running from neck to waist. A purse strap hangs from the gently curved fingers of her right hand, a white handkerchief fanning out from the purse itself.

> upright piano
> faded silence
> of sheet music

I have only my grandmother's word as to who this woman is. Julia Riebschlaeger Bruns, Grandma's mother, second wife to my widowed great-grandfather. She has a name, but little more. One death—mine is near enough—and this photograph could easily fall into a discard pile, into a box of unidentified vintage photos in a dusty junk store somewhere.

> mirror
> patchy with frayed silver
> carnelian cameo profile

ii.
The other photo shows my great-grandfather in a straight-back chair parked at the rear bumper of a car I place in the late thirties. The foreground a bare dirt yard. At the left edge, the wall of an outbuilding. Directly behind the man we called Opa, a glimpse of farmland.

> craggy bark
> on the gnarled live oak
> doves coo among branches

Wilhelm Bruns looks like a composite of the elderly men I knew as a child in the mid-fifties—black wool, white shirt, thin gray hair, face and hands that speak of hard work, hard times.

scent of carnations
earth shoveled
into the open grave

Frayed Thread

Instead of chiding and cajoling, instead of forcing Opa into an old age home or a round of spare beds in their homes . . . though perhaps my grandmother and her siblings pushed these solutions at their father before the hospital released him. But I like to think they didn't. Besides, this is my story. My grandmother, my great-aunts and -uncles—they are my characters, twice removed from the threadbare rehash I dispatch here. Twice a fiction, twice removed by time. Basics disclosed by my grandmother years after the fact—and tapped into a keyboard decades later by this not-yet-born minor character in the story at hand.

>   sitting in his lap
>   wool and mothballs
>   pipe tobacco, cloves

What Grandma, Uncle Anton, Uncle Willie, and Aunt 'Dele accomplished was at once simple and remarkable. They drove a flatbed truck to Opa's place and loaded his little house. They drove the loaded truck along narrow country roads. I like to imagine field hands pausing to gape at the apparition of a house moving through the countryside, raising a wake of dust. Reaching Uncle Anton's place, they set Opa's house down in the backyard. Opa lived there quite contentedly—until April 30, 1953, four months past my fourth birthday.

>   cool fall air
>   at the window
>   his pocket watch stops

Here and Gone

No map can take you there, not to the chairs
                beneath chinaberry trees out back,

your father's voice, your mother's, mingling
                in warm shade, late summer

grazing field dried out, sunshine spilling
                from a bale of hay split open, hunger

dancing in the gathered cows.
                No arrow marks packed earth

of the outer yard where celebrating
                kinfolk parked, cousins spilling

from the Kieschnicks' station wagon,
                Uncle Wilton's two-tone Bel Air.

No map can take you there. To one September afternoon
                your father's voice, your uncles'—

like muffled carom shots around
                the pit, the bed of coals.

Your place in line at the beer keg,
                your plate of sizzling mutton.

No path to the dessert table,
                toothsome syllables

of chocolate · marshmallow · pecan
                —your tongue singing praises

to a bowl of ice cream,
                Sophie Thormahlen's legendary recipe.

Spoons luminescing in late sun.
                The music of Aunt Madeline's laughter.

The coordinates, the measurements
                      have not changed. The mile you drive

down the county road is the same
                      distance as the mile you drove

before. You turn into a hundred
                      acres as before. No need to knock,

no way to enter. The rooms
                      are occupied by strangers now.

Among the Stones

for Lana Meischen Wostal

Her husband's
heart stopped beating yester-
day.

His breath stopped.
Her breath held, her own heart waiting,
his heart silent.

His heart,
her heart, theirs—
no longer keeping time
together.

~~~

Tomorrow
she will rise alone. What
will

she do with-
out him beside her breathing? This
man. This one. Gone.

Alvin
is the name
that will be carved in stone.
His name. Hers.

~~~

So quiet
here among the stones. Here,
where

soon, too soon
she will rest among the others—
father, mother,

husband,
brother—her
kin gone on before. They
promise: *Soon.*

~~~

What to do
with her days until then?
Faith

stronger than
a beating heart, she prays. Lifted
up she rises,

at peace
among her
kin. She knows while her heart
beats, they bide.

Letter from One Still Counting

I'm old now. Let me tell you
what it's like. To rise from bed,
to straighten from bending.
The lower spine catches, Gary,
slowed by an ache that seeped in
while I was busy not paying attention—
the stoop we aped watching grandpas
unbend. Just minutes ago. Trust me on this:
six decades since you and I were young together: fast
as glancing elsewhere. The body catches up, Gary.
Some mornings balance takes a leave, some
mornings my feet refuse the gait I think
is mine to command. The mirror shames
me when I undress to shower: my legs
pale, spindly, spider-veined. Old.

I don't know what happened to you
when you stopped breathing, except
you stopped
         breathing.
                     I know what
they buried. And where. I have known
the stillness there, though for minutes only. Not
years of silence etched by dust and wind,
by caliche crunching beneath tires
when they come to bury what remains of others.

I have always counted, Gary: when you were born,
when I was born—month, day, year—numbers
inscribed on your gravestone,
         your father's . . .
                  his father's . . .
        I count years for those
     among the breathing too.
My number approaches 75. Yours stopped at 33.
Do you count, Gary? Do you miss getting beered up?
         Did you wake for a split second
    when your car drifted into the railing?

Or longer, after, when your heart and breath had stopped?

Is there an after, Gary? I don't know where you are.

Vanishing Point, 1949

Judi is six months past her second birthday
and three steps up the ladder, all dressed up

for company. Crisp white blouse, pressed plaid jumper.
Freshly brushed hair. No coat on this December day.

Raised up on hind legs, two dogs, white-socked
forepaws, are reaching where she climbs, snouts pointing,

alert. One cat perches, silvered gray in faded black
and white, spine arched along the rung Judi has reached

with her hands. The other cat is two rungs farther
up, mid-step coming down. White vest. White forepaws.

My sister has turned toward whoever holds
the camera. But not her eyes. Her eyes look out

past the right edge of the frame. There were pomegranate
shrubs in that direction, a row of them. Pigpens. A thicket

of trees and scrub, a few cows, their meandering trails. Vanished.
But Judi is here, her eyes drawn to something I will never see.

Summer of a Lonesome Farmer

I dream my name in a book of the dead.
Through hot days of August the corn ripens.

    Hot days harden the kernels of August.
    The rattler's brittle tail pulsates a name,

my lot foretold by the brittle tail, rattling.
Calloused fingertips on the barn's tin siding.

    In shade beside the barn calloused fingertips touch.
    I am watermelon. I feed the yellowjackets.

Watermelon glistens. Yellowjackets drink.
They buzz to their nests on dried out cornstalks.

    Black widows, too, nest on dried out cornstalks.
    Summer spills through the hourglass, a red burn.

The days are burning, the hourglass near empty.
I dream my name in a book of the dead.

Qué Será, Será

She doesn't mind the time he spends
in the domino hall downtown, silent
staccato of light and shadow radiating
from fanblades overhead. She listens

to the whir of her Singer, watches
the gleaming needle stitch up yards
of satin the color of ripe plums, muted
voices from *Our Gal Sunday,* its serial quest

for happiness reaching her against
the open-window backdrop of sparrows
in the hackberries, a cow nuzzling
chain-link at the gatepost, honeymoon memory

of blackberry wine on her lips, cool sea breezes
on the balcony of the Casa Ricardo, though beer
is the beverage she shares with Elwood late
afternoons beneath the chinaberry trees out back,

good solid German beer, foam cascading
icy bottles like surf flung up an English cliff
in a poem she memorized in high school, struck
by an emptiness she knew but could not name,

sunless-February counterpoint to a feathered hat,
a pair of patent leather ankle-strap heels
in the window at Lichtenstein's. She walked
right in and tried them on, risked Elwood's gloom

and brought them home. This afternoon, while he
plays dominoes in town, she sews a dress for herself,
sings fragments of a Doris Day song from the movie
they saw last week at the Rialto, a voice to match

the open landscape outside her windows: cottonfields
ripening all the way to the creek, thunderheads dark
in the distance, and the sheen of late-afternoon sun
against satin rippling toward her Singer's needle.

High Cotton

She took the box from the closet,
sat down on the bed with the box

on her lap, removed the lid, reached
into yellowed tissue, and withdrew

a single dress shoe, an open-toed sling-back
pump the color of communion wine—

the dusky blush of it deep down
inside the chalice—a match for the suit

she tailored that fall with the cotton fields
behind her, heat and dust put out of mind,

work gloves, sunbonnet, washed and put
away, a little money in the bank, a morning

spent downtown at Lichtenstein's among
the mannequins, the shoppers, the shoes.

Twenty-four dollars she paid, with the cotton
sold at a hundred a bale—seeds combed out,

hulls thrust aside, the lovely fiber bound and sold—
shoes keeping until she opened the box

and slipped them on, leather straps glowing
ripe against the sheen of seamless nylons,

arched feet, gloved hands, the perfect
suit and hat, all saved, all put away—

shoes nestled in their box on the floor
of the closet while the decades spilled.

The Shapes of Hats

Valerie wore a turban during chemo, her scalp bare
and cool beneath its silky furrows, no wig
to horde the Gulf's close heat. Except
for the trail of oxygen tubes, the wheeled canister
beside her in the dresser mirror's muted glow,
she might have been a Vanderbilt on holiday
all those years ago. Or Nonnie Dougherty rising
out of memory perfectly coifed and hatted, Nonnie
Dougherty rising for communion, the sheen
of her wool suit, her perfect pumps
on the first Sunday of Advent, St. John of the Cross,
1959. Valerie missed the shapes of hats. A felt cloche
her mother wore in 1924, its deep bell-shaped
crown, the brim's sassy arc, tipped down
to the iris of her right eye. A seagreen satin pillbox
she coveted once in the window at Lichtenstein's,
netted veil stippled with tiny puffs of green,
blue roses in outline stitched into the weave
beneath. And yes, the flat-crowned, wide-brimmed
extravagance Madeline bought that day and wore
to sunrise service, Easter Sunday, 1960,
its white straw dappled with silk pansies,
and thick beneath, her hair, like burnished dawn.

Shortly Before the Last Day

The vase opens her mouth as morning wakes.
She makes an O of surprise. Sun spills
through the near window and the vase sings
her single scintillant note. Listen.

She forms an O of delight as sun spills
over rumpled chenille, pours onto polished oak,
a single note, almost too bright. Listen:
someone's mother is breathing her last

under rumpled chenille. Floors of polished oak
harbor secrets of the house, the room, the bed.
Someone's mother is breathing her last.
Beside her, the vase swallows her own shadow.

Who can keep their secrets—house, room, bed,
table—these petals fallen, their fading perfume,
the vase that held them swallowing shadow?
She too is dry. She cannot quench a choking thirst.

Her fallen petals fade. Their bouquet lingers
in the fading woman's dream of flight. Her cup
is dry. It cannot quench her thirsting roses.
Waking, she drinks the day like water

from the cup in her fading dream of light
through the near window while the vase sings.
Awake now, someone's mother drinks the light,
her morning astir, her vase an open mouth.

Dreams of My Mother, 1995

Night before last I was with you again.
We sat together in thick gray winter gloom,
a socked-in sky outside the farmhouse windows.

You took my arm and we walked. Last night
everything was bright. You wore one of your
Jackie Kennedy suits, and you walked between

banks of flowers, you moved toward a cluster
of men in dark suits with one hand in their
pockets: that casual posture we put on

at masses for the dead, letting everyone
know we're men. You've come to let us know
it's all right. You embrace a cousin,

your white-gloved hand against the sheen
at the nape of his neck before you turn and
collapse, the breath flown out of you, a sack

of earth and bones that will not budge.
I stoop with Daddy to drag you from the chapel
but already you are too much for us and

Daddy's voice comes at me like a prophet.
I am my father's son, grief stronger than this weight
that surges, shaking me like prayer, like tears.

This morning my dream is back, your voice
coloring sun that filters through the blinds
as I slip my feet over the bedside and sit up.

When I saw you in April, the sun was out
again. I sat by your dresser watching you polish
your nails, meticulous to the end. You bent

over the task and talked to me: it's your voice
I'm afraid of losing. Not the words we erased
from the message machine after your breath stopped.

No, something else, a fragile thing I cannot
name. It's in the room with me this morning.
My breath catches in the cool fall air.

Habit raises me from the bed and as I take
a first step toward the day, whatever
is there, it flutters and you're gone.

Dry Spell

Ants arrive in June and strip the oleanders.
Corn leaves curl and kernels shrivel, ruining
themselves with aflatoxin. Mornings, Elwood walks

the pasture, dew catching light in parched grass
and muddying dirt on his boots. Hefting the heavy-
bladed grubbing hoe, he severs scrub mesquite trees

at the root. Others hold on, taproots deep enough
to suck up water and turn sunlight green. They wait,
sharp-tipped, like prickly pear and Spanish daggers.

When heat bends the Gulf-thick glare, he walks
back to the house, hangs the grubbing hoe in its place
on the tractor shed wall, and sits beneath hackberries,

remembering. Queen's wreath rustles against
the rumble of trucks on the highway, tempered
by distance and sparrows. As a boy, Elwood watched

the highway unfold. They used mules to raise up
the roadbed, fed them Johnson-grass hay, seed drifting
along the Agua Dulce, runners burrowing after rainfall.

Inside, he turns on the window unit, listens
to the sibilant quiet, a stillness inside amber.
His sons and daughter smile from the walls,

the luster that shines from unlined faces bright
as memory twenty years later. Everything
is where it should be, brass pheasants nesting

beside the couch, sewing machine in its corner
by the window seat, sunlight pooling there.
He drives to town, plays dominoes with men

he's known so long their habits have worn smooth,
so many years of the rough and jocular that grief
can find no voice among them. Back home

he walks through heat turned gray and mild—
inside to his favorite chair. Beside him Valerie's
rocking chair sits empty. Elwood rests a hand

on its smooth polished arm, and pointing the remote,
clicks on television news. He will fall asleep here.
Voices will wake him—and flickering light.

Months Later, He Rises from a Nap

A film of dust on her dresser chair,
beside it her purse. Her mirror

gives back the room—afternoon
shadows, doorway, fading

room beyond. Windows.
The space between breaths.

Stillness battening after the last
breath. Hope trapped in the rib cage.

Waiting. Her breath did not come.
Her purse holds what remains.

Pegasus Leaping

This is a letter to you, Daddy, not yet
grown into yourself, a letter to the hat-brim
shadows masking your eyes, your father's eyes.

This is a letter to the Magnolia station where
you stand—your mother's floral print, your father's
towering figure, two older brothers—to you

as one at home among five, a family. Whole.
This is to the hush of shadow brimming the pickup truck
parked on smooth caliche. This is to Pegasus leaping

atop the gas pumps, to the R.C. Cola sign behind you,
bottles jutting. And the lone train car beyond. This is
a letter to a 1940 summer sky, to age fifteen, a letter

to innocence, to what you don't know
the year ahead will hold. Your father's razor blade.
Your father's blood. Your father breathing his last.

This is a letter to grief, a letter to silence,
to grief silenced. This is to the weight we
will carry in the years to come. This is to silence

inside the roar of tractoring, to hours that shimmer
with heat, with dust. To cotton sack and baled hay,
to posthole digger, milking stanchion, sausage stuffer.

This is for the words I never spoke, working beside
you, your father's death a cleft between us,
my own truth wrapped in silence, no air for us to breathe.

This is a letter to the faded blaze of sun
on your white shirt, to suspenders and white shoes,
to the glint of summer in your buckle. This is a letter

to my daydream for you, Daddy, to hackberry
shade, to the girl I conjure for you there. I even
know her name. I wonder if she is dreaming you.

Lesser Notes

Names

Pronouncing names as their owners say them feels essential to me. My great-grandfather Wilhelm Bruns appears in these pages. Wilhelm, pronounced *Vill-helm*, equal emphasis on both syllables. The vowel in Bruns has an ooh sound. *Broohns*. If you can roll an *r*, you get extra credit for rolling this one. Don't say Bruhns—that's someone else's name.

My great aunt 'Dele was born Adele, but the first syllable was always dropped. We called her simply Aunt *Day-luh*. My family name is Meischen, pronounced *MY-shn*. My mother's family name was Morgenroth, pronounced *MOR-gn-ROTE*.

Hackberry Trees

The operative word here is trees. Hackberries are trees, not bushes or shrubs. They *look* like trees—upright trunks, corrugated bark. They are not known for berries.

Milking

It wasn't until my sister arrived at nursing school that Meischens gave a second thought to this morning routine. After I learned to milk a cow, I would take the milk pail out to the pen, dip it into the water trough, slick with algae and rife with whatever our cows had on their tongues when they drank from it. Next, I set the pail beneath the cow and splashed water onto her udder—often encrusted with dried mud and manure. When the udder and teats were "clean," I sloshed the water around the pail, slung it into the pen, set the pail back under the cow and milked her. Back in the house, we strained the milk into jars, refrigerated it. Drank it. I credit our milk, among other things, with my robust immune system.

The Pentina

"Hurricane Force" originated as a sestina—six stanzas of six lines each, with the same six end words repeating in a spiraling order as the stanzas proceed. A close friend and accomplished poet read the poem and felt that the opening stanza was what my husband Scott would call an onramp. I agreed, but for me the hurricane was over and done at the close of the original sixth stanza. Briefly, I considered a "sestina" of five six-line stanzas, but that didn't feel right. So. I cut the onramp stanza, read the new opening stanza and decided to cut line six—and every succeeding line with the same end word. Doing so meant that the lines of remaining stanzas would be in the wrong order. I wanted end words to repeat as they do in a sestina—bottom to top or outside-in: 5-1-4-2-3. I took each stanza apart, re-ordered the lines according to sestina rules, then plunged in and turned what was left into what I'm calling a pentina. I have rarely had such fun wrestling with words.

Place of Magic

Lichtenstein's (pronounced LITCH-in-STEEN's) was a department store in downtown Corpus Christi. It is well nigh impossible to explain the enchantment inhering in the name itself, let alone the transformation that overpowered rural souls inside its gleaming plate-glass doors. Air conditioned air was . . . well, cool. It was dry. It smelled of perfume and cologne and rich fabrics. Lichtenstein's offered the unprecedented experience of an elevator, the almost queasy sensation of the floor moving beneath your feet as the uniformed operator announced the approaching level. There was a mezzanine, with a view of the ground floor—rack upon rack of beautiful things. No heat here, no dust, no work, no sweat.

Acknowledgments

Big Land, Big Sky, Big Hair (Dos Gatos Press, 2008)
   "Moments from the Dance"

Blood Tree Literature
   "The Algebra of Chance"

Bosque
   "High Cotton"
   "His Hands Know How to Do It"
   "Walking South Texas"

Chaos Dive Reunion (Mutabilis Press, 2023)
   "This Boy"

Cider Press Review
   "The Shapes of Hats"

contemporary haibun online
   "The Rest Is Silence"

Copper Shade Tree
   "Requiem"

di-verse-city
   "Canning Day, 1955"
   "The Garnett Translation"

The Ekphrastic Review
   "What Survives Them"

Equinox
   "Cotton Harvest, 1949"

Glissando (2023 New Mexico State Poetry Society Anthology)
   "A History in Footsteps"
   "Hold Me, Darling, for a Little While"

Impossible Archetype
   "Here and Gone"
   "On a Barstool at the Double Down"

Layers (Plain View Press, 1994)
   "Butcher Day"
   "Valerie"

Naugatuck River Review
   "Another Kind of Answer"
   "In the Cow Shed"
   "Undone"

Peauxdunque Review
   "Cotton Harvest, 1962"
   "Vanishing Point, 1949"

San Pedro River Review
   "After the Harvest: Tractor, Stalk Cutter, Disk Harrow"
   "He Wanted a Straightedge Life"
   "Summer of a Lonesome Farmer"

Southern Poetry Review
   "Midsummer Morning"
   "Qué Será, Será"

Southwestern American Literature
   "What Holds You Here"

Talking Writing
   "Shortly Before the Last Day"

Two Southwests (Virtual Artists Collective, 2008)
   "Dry Spell"

Weaving the Terrain (Dos Gatos Press, 2017)
   "Testament"

Wingbeats II: Exercises and Practice in Poetry (Dos Gatos Press, 2014)
   "As on the First Day"

"Death Wish" and "No Man's Land" are adapted from passages in "Not a Word Among Us," *The Common* (October 2019).

In Appreciation

Heartfelt gratitude first and foremost to my husband, Scott Wiggerman, unexcelled as reader-editor of my poems. Special thanks to Scott for his close attention to the haibun in this collection. Thanks also to Gabrielle Langley, John Milkereit, and Sandi Stromberg for their close attention to the language of the poems, the ordering of the pages. I have the good fortune of two poetry critique groups, who contributed to whatever success these poems achieve: my local poetry group Amy Beveridge, Stan Crawford, Goyo Candela, and—again—Scott Wiggerman; my Zoom poetry group Tina Carlson, Cindy Huyser, Eileen Lawrence, Scott McDaniel, and Radha Marcum. Since August 2020, I've been leading poetry writing classes via Zoom—with poets from all four U.S. time zones. A number of the poems here grew out of these sessions. Space prohibits naming all the participants, but I thank them wholeheartedly—for their energy, their generosity, their insights. Finally, I want to thank Bruce Snider, whose exercise on the notebook poem, drawing on two Pima Road Notebook poems by Keith Ekiss, put "county road poems" into my head and spurred me to complete these pages.

A Pushcart honoree, with a personal essay in *Pushcart Prize XLII*, David Meischen is the author of *Nopalito, Texas: Stories*, new from the University of New Mexico Press. *Anyone's Son*, from 3: A Taos Press, was selected Best First Book of Poetry by the Texas Institute of Letters (TIL). David has twice received the Kay Cattarulla Award for Best Short Story from TIL, most recently for "Crossing at the Light," lead story in his collection, *The Distance Between Here and Elsewhere: Three Stories* (*Storylandia*, 2020). David's work has appeared in *The Common, Copper Nickel, The Gettysburg Review, Naugatuck River Review, The San Pedro River Review, Southern Poetry Review, The Southern Review, Talking Writing, Valparaiso Fiction Review*, and elsewhere. A former juror for the Kimmel Harding Nelson center for the arts, David is an alumnus of the Jentel Arts residency program. Co-founder and managing editor of Dos Gatos Press, he lives in Albuquerque, NM with his husband—also his co-publisher and co-editor—Scott Wiggerman.

www.ingramcontent.com/pod-product-compliance
Lightning Source LLC
Chambersburg PA
CBHW031601170426
43196CB00032B/981